CAESAR RODNEY'S RIDE

CAESAR RODNEY'S RIDE

The Story of an American Patriot

By Jan Cheripko

Illustrated by Gary Lippincott

Boyds Mills Press

To Kent Brown, who understands the importance of the choices we make
—J. C.

To the Revolution
—G. L.

Text copyright © 2004 by Jan Cheripko
Illustrations copyright © 2004 by Gary Lippincott

Published by Boyds Mills Press, Inc.
A Highlights Company
815 Church Street
Honesdale, Pennsylvania 18431
Printed in China
Visit our Web site at: www.boydsmillspress.com

Publisher Cataloging-in-Publication Data (U.S.)

Cheripko, Jan.
    Caesar Rodney's ride : the story of an American patriot / by Jan Cheripko ;
illustrated by Gary Lippincott. —1st ed.
[40] p. : col. ill. ;   cm.
Includes bibliographical references and index.
Summary: The story of Caesar Rodney, who was determined to sign the Declaration of Independence.
ISBN 1-59078-065-5
1. Rodney, Caesar, 1728-1784 — Juvenile literature. 2. Statesmen — United States — Biography — Juvenile
literature. 3. United States — History — Revolution, 1775-1783 — Juvenile literature. 4. United States.
Declaration of Independence — Signers — Biography — Juvenile literature. 5. United States. Continental
Congress — Biography — Juvenile literature. (1. Rodney, Caesar, 1728-1784. 2. Statesmen. 3. United States —
History — Revolution, 1775-1783.) I. Lippincott, Gary A., ill. II. Title.
973.3/092 B 21   E207.R6C54 2004
2004100239

First edition, 2004
The text of this book is set in 16-point Garamond.

10 9 8 7 6 5 4 3 2 1

AUTHOR'S NOTE:

While legend has it that Caesar Rodney wore a "green" scarf, there are no records, letters, or portraits that say or show that the scarf was "green." We have decided to honor the oral tradition.

Years after the signing of the Declaration of Independence, Caesar Rodney's friend wrote that Rodney appeared at the State House the afternoon of July 2 covered in mud and wearing riding boots and spurs. However, Thomas Rodney, Caesar's brother, wrote that Caesar began the ride by calling for a carriage. I have tried to incorporate both accounts. It is clear that Caesar could not have made an eighty-mile ride that quickly in a carriage. And no one horse could have carried him on such a grueling journey overnight.

While there are no known portraits of Caesar Rodney (perhaps because of the unsightly open wound on his face), we have imagined what Caesar Rodney might have looked like in order to make him more real to young readers.

— Jan Cheripko

ACKNOWLEDGMENTS

My grateful appreciation to Greg Linder for his patience and painstaking perseverance to get it right. I would also like to thank the following individuals for their help and expertise:

Josephine Birtwhistle, Royal Naval Museum
George Comtois, Lexington Historical Society
Patsy Copeland, Tulane Medical Library
Karie Diethorn, Colonial National Historic Park
Dr. Robert L. Hewitt, Tulane University Medical School
Greg Johnson, David Library of the American Revolution
Richard Kollen, Lexington Historical Society
Timothy Mullin, Historical Society of Delaware
Matthew Sheldon, Royal Naval Museum
Tom Summers, Delaware Public Archives
Jane Triber, Ph.D.

Lastly, my thanks to Candace Fleming for inspiring this project with her wonderful story of Caesar Rodney that appeared in *Highlights for Children* magazine.

Map of Pennsylvania(1776) reprinted by permission of Harold Cramer, Historical Maps of Pennsylvania, www.mapsofpa.com.

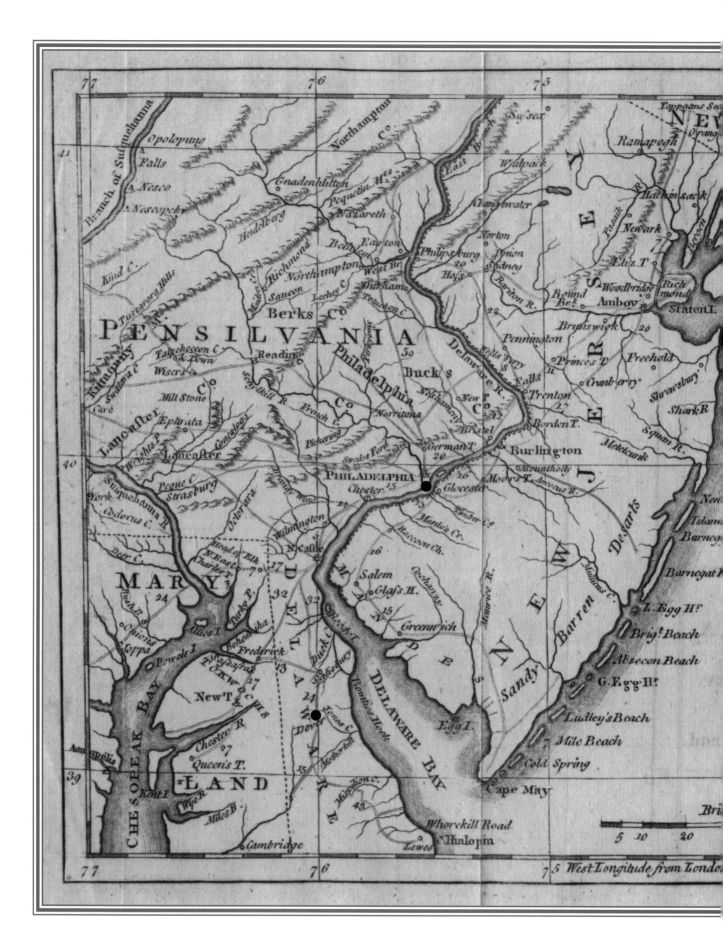

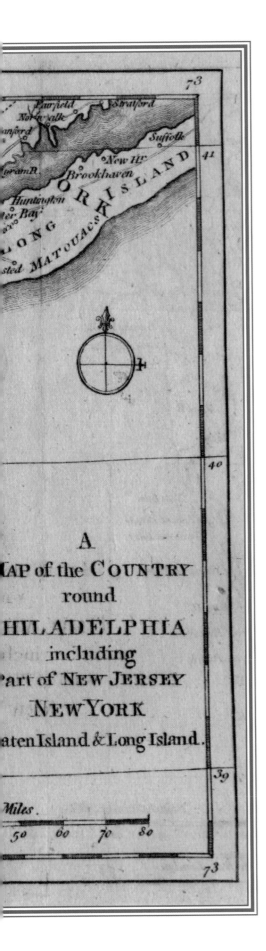

A
MAP of the COUNTRY
round
PHILADELPHIA
including
Part of NEW JERSEY
NEW YORK
Staten Island & Long Island.

Miles.

This map of the "Country round Philadelphia" appeared in the September 1776 issue of *Gentlemen's Magazine: and Historical Chronicle,* published in London, England.

Though small in territory, Delaware had a great impact on the formation of the United States. Caesar Rodney, one of Delaware's representatives to the Second Continental Congress, cast a critical vote for independence. Later, in 1787, Delaware was the first to ratify the United States Constitution. For this reason, Delaware is known as "The First State."

The dots, which have been superimposed on the original map, show Dover, which is near Caesar Rodney's home, and Philadelphia, the site of the Second Continental Congress.

THE MESSAGE CAME TO CAESAR RODNEY on the hot, sticky afternoon of July 1, 1776. Thomas McKean, fellow delegate from the new state of Delaware, was begging Caesar Rodney to return at once to Philadelphia. Rodney read the words, then called for his carriage.

Proclamations from King George III and tax laws passed by Parliament fueled the move for independence in the colonies.

The Proclamation of 1763
Fighting broke out in the Ohio Valley when settlers entered the lands of the Chippewa, Shawnee, and Delaware tribes. King George declared that any white settlers who ventured west of the Allegheny Mountains would not be protected by English soldiers. Many white settlers ignored the proclamation.

A letter summoning Caesar Rodney back to Philadelphia arrived on July 1, 1776.

Caesar began a journey that would alter the course of history.

At the Philadelphia State House, delegates to the Second Continental Congress were about to risk their properties, their families, and their own lives in a historic decision. Should the thirteen American colonies declare their independence from King George and Great Britain? Caesar Rodney strongly believed they should. As one of Delaware's three Congressional delegates, he would ride to cast his vote for independence.

The Sugar Act, 1764
Keeping soldiers in the colonies cost money. England tried to raise the funds by taxing sugar. The colonists didn't think England had a right to tax them. As a result, sugar came into the colonies smuggled aboard ships. The British navy could not stop the smugglers. The Sugar Act failed.

CAESAR CLIMBED INTO HIS CARRIAGE, yelled to the horse, and raced north toward Philadelphia, some eighty miles away. He would have to ride all afternoon in the scorching July heat, then continue on through the night, reaching the State House sometime the next day. As his Kent County plantation faded in the distance behind him, clouds of fine dust from the dry roads filled the carriage. Caesar coughed and hoped he wouldn't give in to another attack of asthma, which sometimes left him gasping for breath. Instinctively, he pulled his green scarf tighter to protect the open wound below his eye caused by the cancer that slowly ate away at his face. But Caesar had other thoughts besides his personal battle with asthma and cancer.

The Stamp Act, 1765
After the failure of the Sugar Act, England tried to raise money by taxing official documents such as mortgages, licenses, and wills. Colonists were so vehemently opposed to the tax that officials were unwilling to enforce the Stamp Act.

Eighty miles separated Caesar and his vote for independence.

The blood of American patriots and English soldiers had been spilled in 1775.

WAR BETWEEN THE COLONIES and Great Britain was threatening. The blood of American patriots and English soldiers had been spilled more than a year earlier at Lexington and Concord. Another battle had occurred in Quebec the previous December, and only last June British and colonial forces had met on Breed's Hill in Boston. The American patriots had fought valiantly during the battle, turning back several attacks by British soldiers. But when the patriots ran out of ammunition, they were forced to flee. The fight, which mistakenly came to be known as the Battle of Bunker Hill, had cost the British dearly. More than one thousand English soldiers were killed or wounded. One year after the battle, the patriots had forced the British to abandon Boston. It was a humiliating defeat for the great empire of Britain.

The Declaratory Act, 1766
This act declared that England had the right to tax the colonies whenever the king and Parliament wanted. The colonists might have won the battle over the Stamp Act, but the war over taxation was far from over.

Now, as Caesar rode, an English battle fleet, filled with several thousand soldiers thirsting for revenge against the colonists, was sailing toward Long Island. There, General George Washington and the patriots he commanded anxiously waited to fight in a war that had not yet been officially declared.

The Townsend Acts, 1767
Charles Townsend, a member of Parliament, was the author of these acts that taxed tea and other goods such as paint and glass. Samuel Adams sent a letter to all the colonies condemning the acts. British officials demanded that the colonists condemn Adams. Instead, the colonists refused to buy British goods. The taxes were repealed. The tax on tea, however, remained.

British frigates brought more than 15,000 soldiers to Long Island, and bottled up merchant ships in New York City.

The Men

Here are some of the major historical figures who played important roles in the story of independence.

Samuel Adams

Perhaps more than any other colonial American, Samuel Adams was responsible for the start of the Revolutionary War. He spoke out often and passionately, and was the organizing force behind the Boston Tea Party.

John Adams

John Adams, cousin of Samuel Adams, was a leader in the push for independence. A lawyer and philosopher, he helped to found the republic. He was the first vice-president of the United States under George Washington, and second President of the new nation.

John Dickinson

A man of high principle, John Dickinson battled both Samuel Adams and John Adams. He led the anti-independence faction of the Pennsylvania delegation to the Second Continental Congress. Though he refused to sign the Declaration of Independence, he enlisted in the Continental Army.

King George III

When George III came to the throne, England was caught in a costly war with France and Spain. The colonists called it the French and Indian War. England won the war, but the cost was enormous. To help pay for the debt, George III decided to tax the colonies.

George Washington

He commanded the Continental Army, managing to hold the troops together in the darkest times of the war. Washington, the Father of Our Country, became the first President of the United States.

One of delegates from Delaware, Thomas McKean, argued for independence.

A vote for independence would mean war; a vote to remain loyal to King George would mean a future of unfair laws and unreasonable taxes imposed by King George. To many colonists, the king seemed determined to impoverish his American subjects in order to pay for his past wars against France and Spain. Others, called Loyalists, felt that the colonies should remain loyal to the king and to England. The outcome of the vote was anything but certain, so Caesar hoped desperately to reach the State House in time.

Tiny Delaware had only recently seceded from Pennsylvania. Delaware's new assembly sent three delegates to the Second Continental Congress in Philadelphia. One of its delegates was Thomas McKean, a Scottish-Irish attorney who stood in favor of independence. The second delegate, George Read, was also an attorney, but he opposed breaking from Great Britain. Caesar, who had returned to Delaware to put down a rebellion by Loyalists, regarded both men as his friends. However, he sided with McKean on the issue of independence. But if Caesar wasn't in Philadelphia in time for the vote, McKean's vote for independence would be canceled by Read's vote against it. Delaware would remain deadlocked, and the cause of independence would be weakened.

The Intolerable Acts, 1774

Colonists in Boston responded to the tax on tea by dumping tea into the harbor in what is known as the Boston Tea Party. England struck back with a series of acts that closed Boston Harbor until the tea and the tax on tea were paid for. The acts also forced colonists to house British soldiers in their homes. Delegates from all the colonies met in Philadelphia in a Continental Congress to determine what they should do next.

Tired and choking on dust that was making his asthma worse, Caesar rode on, his ever-present green scarf covering the open wound on his face.

Caesar was a young man when he developed a cancerous sore on the left side of his face. It soon spread from the bottom of his eye to his nose, and Caesar was keenly aware of how ugly the open wound looked to others. He almost always covered his face with a green scarf, and no likeness of him was ever drawn or painted. Fellow delegate John Adams once described Caesar as ". . . the oddest looking man in the world; he is tall, thin, and slender as a reed, pale; his face is not bigger than a large apple, yet there is a sense and fire, spirit, wit, and humor in his countenance."

BATTLES AND WAR
A number of historical events led to the American Revolution.

The French and Indian War, 1756-1763
War broke out when France and England both laid claim to territory in the Ohio Valley. The conflict spread to Europe, where it became known as the Seven Years War. In America, it was known as the French and Indian War because the Indians fought on the side of France. England won the war, gaining most of the lands east of the Mississippi River, but the financial cost was high. King George taxed the colonies to pay for the war.

". . . tall, thin, and slender as a reed" is how John Adams described Caesar Rodney.

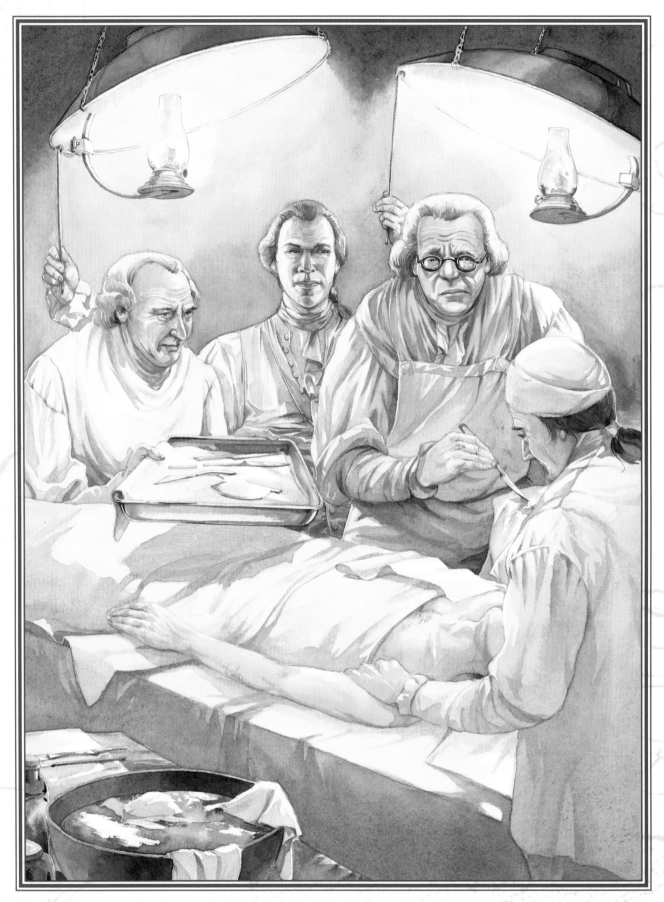

The surgery was "a dreadful undertaking."

As the trouble between the colonies and Great Britain grew more serious, Caesar's cancer also worsened. Doctors told Caesar that the best they could do for him was to perform surgery to remove the cancerous portion of his face. Caesar wrote to his brother Thomas, saying he regarded such surgery as "a dreadful undertaking." Even this radical operation offered no assurance of a cure. Some doctors advised Caesar to travel immediately to England, where better treatments might be available. Thomas and many of Caesar's friends also urged him to go to England.

It was not easy for Caesar to accept any sort of help from the English. He deeply resented the oppression by the king, and believed that the colonies should sever ties with Great Britain. He knew he might face danger in England, as well. As tensions between Britain and the colonies grew, a trip by Caesar to England might end in his imprisonment, or even in his execution as a traitor. Caesar decided to have his cancer treated in Philadelphia. The surgery left a hole in his face, exposing bone and extending from the corner of his left eye halfway down his nose.

The Boston Massacre, March 5, 1770
Each of England's taxation acts made the colonists angrier. Tensions had been mounting in Boston for weeks. Finally, they exploded in what Samuel Adams called the Boston Massacre. British soldiers, harassed and taunted by hundreds of Bostonians, fired on the crowd, killing four civilians, and wounding six.

Unfortunately, the "dreadful undertaking" did not cure Caesar's cancer. As he rode through an increasingly violent thunderstorm, now on horseback, he knew his vote would make him unwelcome in England, the only place he thought he might get help for the cancer. Caesar Rodney knew he was on his way to signing his own death sentence.

Meanwhile, in Philadelphia, delegate John Dickinson rose to speak. A Quaker and wealthy merchant from Pennsylvania, Dickinson was another friend of Caesar Rodney's. Years earlier Dickinson had written an anti-British pamphlet called *Letters from a Farmer in Pennsylvania*, condemning the Townsend Acts. But in July of 1776, he didn't think the colonists stood a chance of winning a war against Great Britain. As the head of the Pennsylvania delegation, Dickinson had been doing everything he could to prevent a vote in favor of independence.

The Boston Tea Party, December 16, 1773
Approximately 5,000 Bostonians assembled at the harbor to protest the tea tax. They would not permit ships to unload their tea. An organization called the Sons of Liberty, organized by Samuel Adams, boarded the ships. Dressed as Mohawk Indians, the men dumped more than 90,000 pounds of tea into Boston Harbor.

As John Adams spoke in favor of independence, Caesar Rodney rode through a violent thunderstorm

To declare independence would be "like destroying our house in winter. . . ."

Sometime during the afternoon of July 1, as the temperature climbed, Dickinson rose to convince the delegates at the State House that his position was the wisest one. The air hung heavy with the oppressive summer heat. John Adams, his cousin Samuel Adams, John Hancock, Benjamin Franklin, and others in favor of independence watched nervously as Dickinson argued strongly against independence, telling the delegates what they already knew: A war with England would mean fighting the Indians, too, because the British would arm the tribes and encourage them to attack. A war, Dickinson reminded them, would bring down the full force of the English army and navy, the strongest in the world at the time. By comparison, the colonies had no trained army, no navy, and very few weapons. Dickinson hammered the weary men with facts. The colonists had very little money to support a war. No one knew whether the colonial soldiers would even fight against the experienced British troops and the feared Hessian soldiers of Germany. Like steam rising in the blazing afternoon sun from the Delaware River nearby, the desire for independence seemed to evaporate in the heat of Dickinson's burning words.

Dickinson told them that they could not count on the support of France, the other great European power. He reminded the delegates that the British had recently routed colonial soldiers in Canada, that George Washington's ragtag forces faced imminent attack in New York, and that South Carolina was under siege as he spoke. To declare independence now, Dickinson warned, would be "like destroying our house in winter and exposing a growing family before we have got another shelter."

Dickinson's words drifted to the roof of the meeting room, soft like a haunting echo warning of a coming disaster. The message was clear: Once the delegates voted for independence, there was no turning back. The colonists would be alone after that. Alone in their struggle against the great might of England. Alone in a bitter and savage battle against the Indians. Alone in a fight against their neighbors, friends and family members who sided with England. If the colonists voted for war, a war that seemed impossible to win, all of the men who voted for independence at the State House on this hot day in July would be caught, put in jail, tried for treason, and hanged.

John Dickinson sat down; his words lay heavy in the minds of the delegates. Most had grown up thinking of themselves as loyal English subjects. Now they would be traitors. Men fidgeted nervously waiting for someone to speak. Some wiped their foreheads with already sweat-soaked shirtsleeves and glanced at each other, wondering who would rise to argue against Dickinson. Still, no one spoke. Perhaps Dickinson was right. Maybe there was no argument strong enough and they should stop this nonsense about independence. But if the colonies were going to break free from the tyranny of England, then someone had to stand and denounce Dickinson's arguments. Urged by others, John Adams, the outspoken patriot from Boston, rose to speak.

Adams was not a tall, imposing man like the six-feet-two-inch George Washington. And compared to his fiery cousin Samuel Adams, who had been protesting against the British for more than two decades, John Adams was a relative newcomer to the cause of independence. But he was an eloquent and persuasive speaker. In fact, after the Boston Massacre, it was John Adams who argued successfully against his cousin Samuel Adams and others in defense of the British soldiers who had fired on the unruly Boston mob. Thanks to John Adams, the soldiers were cleared of the charge of murder.

The hot July sun that had baked the room all afternoon was slipping into dusk beyond the distant mountains when Adams rose to speak. Evening blanketed the city of Philadelphia, and an eerie silence had descended on the delegates to the Second Continental Congress. The tension in the State House mounted, and huge storm clouds, black and threatening, rolled into Philadelphia.

As the words of John Adams filled the hearts and minds of the delegates, the hot summer sky erupted in an explosion of sound and sight that seemed as if the war had begun and the city itself was being bombarded by the British. Lightning illuminated the chamber. Thunder rocked its walls. John Adams looked like one of his Puritan ancestors preaching about hell and damnation. His words stung the hearts and minds of the delegates, challenging them to do what was right and true, and giving them the power to do a supernatural thing — vote for independence even though all the logic of the world told them that to do so would be hopeless.

Though Adams did not remember what he said, nor did anyone write it down, Thomas Jefferson later recalled that Adams "came out with a power of thought and expression that moved us from our seats."

At last John Adams sat down. Virginia's Benjamin Harrison asked for a trial vote to determine where the delegates stood. They would now vote for or against a resolution proposed by Virginia delegate Richard Henry Lee, whose brave words declared that "these United Colonies are free and independent states . . . that all political connection between them and the State of Great Britain is, and ought to be, totally dissolved."

On July 4, 1776, Congress adopted the Declaration of Independence.

The Battles of Lexington and Concord, April 18-19, 1775
*British troops headed to Lexington to destroy the local militia's guns and
ammunition. On their way, they encountered a group of militia called
minutemen. The minutemen dispersed, and the British marched to Concord.
In Concord, the colonists stood their ground and fought. The British retreated,
returning to Boston, beaten and humiliated. The war for independence had begun.*

The roll call began with the northernmost colony of New Hampshire, which voted "yea" for independence. The last colony to cast its vote was the southern colony of Georgia, which also supported the resolution. All in all, nine colonies favored independence, while Pennsylvania and South Carolina were opposed. New York's delegates did not vote because they had received no direction from their assembly. Delaware, the newest and second-smallest colony, was deadlocked, with delegate Thomas McKean in favor, delegate George Read opposed, and Caesar Rodney still absent.

Majority support for independence was not enough. The Congressional leaders believed that all of the colonies must agree if they were to stand a chance of winning the war. After the trial vote, Adams, Jefferson, Ben Franklin, John Hancock, Thomas Payne, and others talked to the delegates from Pennsylvania and South Carolina, hoping to change their minds. New York's delegates already favored independence, but they would continue to abstain until they received directions from their colonial government.

Payne and Franklin began to sway the Pennsylvania delegates. John Dickinson could see that Adams's speech had successfully countered his arguments. He and Robert Morris, another opponent of independence, decided to be absent during the final vote. Pennsylvania would join the others in voting for freedom. Adams's speech had so moved the South Carolina delegates that, against the direction of their own government, they also declared themselves ready to support independence. As for Delaware, somehow Caesar Rodney had to return to Philadelphia in time to vote.

As his neighbor John Dickinson argued against independence, Caesar raced north from his home in St. Jones Neck to vote for it. In the scorching July heat of the afternoon he rode through Dover onto the King's Highway, then across Duck's Creek and Appoquinimink Creek, and north to New Castle, the state capital. On he rode to Wilmington, then took the ferry across the Christina River, and the bridge across the Brandywine River

Against the backdrop of the flashing light and booming thunder of a summer storm, the words of John Adams had lifted the minds of the delegates to majestic heights. But for Caesar Rodney the burst that tore open the sky battered him mercilessly as he rode toward Philadelphia. In the black night through thunder, lightning, and torrential rain, he rode. Somewhere north of Dover, he left his carriage behind and continued on horseback. Astride his mount, he pounded down dirt roads that had become little more than mud wallows. He crossed on battered bridges over swollen creeks, and raced through towns on slick cobblestone streets.

On the afternoon of July 2, his legs raw and beaten from riding, his face whipped by the wind and rain, his back sore from galloping hour after hour, Caesar arrived in Philadelphia. Covered with mud and dust and still wearing his riding boots and spurs, Caesar met his friend Thomas McKean at the foot of the State House. The two walked up the steps and turned into a large room filled with men from all thirteen colonies. Some sat at tables, others leaned against the wall or the railing. All listened as the final debate on independence came to a close.

A monument to Caesar Rodney stands in Christ Church, Dover, Delaware.

The time had come. The second vote for independence — the vote that would bind them together in victory or lead to their destruction — was about to start. The roll call began: New Hampshire again supported independence, as did Massachusetts, Connecticut, and Rhode Island. New York abstained. New Jersey voted in favor. Now it was Delaware's turn.

Delegate Thomas McKean voted yes; delegate George Read voted no. Then Caesar Rodney rose to speak. It was later written that Rodney spoke these words: "As I believe the voice of my constituents and of all sensible and honest men is in favor of independence, my own judgment concurs with them. I vote for independence."

Maryland, Virginia, North Carolina, South Carolina, and Georgia followed, with not a negative vote among them. Twelve colonies had voted, and the decision was unanimous. (Even New York cast its support behind the resolution by the time the Declaration of Independence was signed on August 2, 1776.) Two days after the roll-call vote, on July 4, 1776, Congress adopted the official Declaration of Independence. Caesar Rodney, Thomas McKean, and George Read signed the Declaration, but Pennsylvania's John Dickinson did not. The vote meant independence—at least for now. It also meant going to war with the most powerful army and navy in the world.

Now the War for Independence began in earnest. Throughout the summer of 1776, the British chased George Washington's army out of Long Island and New York City, then across the Hudson River into New Jersey, and into Pennsylvania beyond the Delaware. For the next seven years, the delegates and many thousands of colonists would pay a heavy price for their courage.

During the war, Caesar served as Major General of the Delaware State Militia. However, as the conflict dragged on, his health deteriorated. By the time the formal peace treaty between the new United States and Great Britain was signed in 1783, Caesar was too sick with cancer to participate in the celebration.

Shortly thereafter, the Delaware State Assembly voted to begin meeting at Rodney's home, fifteen miles from the state capital. Legislators took this action to honor all that Caesar had done for Delaware and for the country. He was now the speaker of the assembly and the "president" of Delaware, in effect acting as the state's governor.

The assembly met at Rodney's house for the last time on April 8, 1784. In late June, barely more than a year after King George III had signed the treaty ending the War for Independence, Caesar died of cancer. He was buried on his plantation, in an unmarked grave. Caesar's remains lay in that humble grave for more than a century. In 1889, a monument was erected in his honor at Christ Church in Dover.

For casting an important vote, for signing the Declaration of Independence, for his military service during the War of Independence, for holding more public offices than any Delaware citizen before or since, Caesar is remembered. But it is his courageous eighty-mile ride for freedom that has made Caesar Rodney "the hero of Delaware."

SUGGESTED READING

Gregory, Kris. *The Winter of Red Snow*. New York, NY: Scholastic, 1996.

Harness, Cheryl. *George Washington*. Washington, DC: National Geographic, 2000.

Issacs, Sally Senzell. *America in the Time of George Washington: 1747 to 1803*. Des Plaines, Ill.: Heineman Library, 1998.

Klingel, Cynthia, & Robert B. Noyed. *Paul Revere's Ride*. Chanhassen, MN: Child's World, 2002.

Klingel, Cynthia, & Robert B. Noyed. *The Revolutionary War*. Chanhassen, MN: Child's World, 2002.

Kroll, Steven. *The Boston Tea Party*. New York, NY: Holiday House, 1998.

Masoff, Joy. *American Revolution*. New York, NY: Scholastic, 2000.

Osborne, Mary Pope. *Revolutionary War on Wednesday*. New York, NY: Random House Boosk for Young Readers, 2000.

Peacock, Louise. *Crossing the Delaware*. New York, NY: Simon and Schuster,1998.

Yoder, Carolyn P. (Ed.). *George Washington, the Writer*. Honesdale, PA: Boyds Mills Press, 2003.

SOURCES

Axelrod, Dr. Alan, and Charles Phillips, *What Every American Should Know About History: 200 Events That Shaped the Nation*. Holbrook, MA: Adams Media Corporation, 1992.

Burnett, Edmund Cody. *The Continental Congress*. New York, NY: The Macmillan Company, 1941.

Cheripiko, Jan. *Voices of the River: Adventures on the Delaware*. Honesdale, PA: Boyds Mills Press, 1993.

Churchill, Winston S. *A History of the English Speaking Peoples*. New York, NY: Dodd, Mead and Company, 1956.

Crystal, David. *The Cambridge Biographical Encyclopedia*. New York, NY: The Cambridge University Press, 1994.

Emory, Noemie. *Washington: A Biography*. New York, NY: Putnam, 1976.

Fast, Howard. *The Crossing*. New York, NY: Simon and Schuster, 1999.

Fenimore, Harvey Curtis, Jr. *Delaware's Symbols, Slogan, Name, and Nicknames*. Dover, DE: Dover Post Company, 1990.

Fenimore, Harvey Curtis, Jr. *Delaware's Beginnings: The Earliest Settlers*. Dover, DE: Finmere Books, 1994.

Fleming, Thomas. *1776: Year of Illusions*. New York: NY: W.W. Norton, 1975.

Fleming, Thomas; *Liberty!* New York, NY: Viking Penquin Press, 1997.

Frank, William P. *Caesar Rodney, Patriot*. Wilmington, DE: Delaware American Revolution Bicentennial Commission, 1975

Hancock, Harold B. *The Loyalists of Revolutionary Delaware*. Newark, DE: University of Delaware Press, 1977.

Harness, Cheryl. *George Washington*. Washington, D.C.: National Geographic Society, 2000.

Hawke, David Freeman. *Honorable Treason: The Declaration of Independence and the Men Who Signed It*. New York, NY: The Viking Press, 1976.

Hawke, David Freeman. *A Transaction of Free Men: The Birth and Course of the Declaration of Independence*. New York, NY: Charles Scribner's Sons, 1964.

Hoffecker, Carol E., Ph.D. *Delaware, the First State*. Wilmington, DE: Middle Atlantic Press, 1988.

Josephy, Alvin M., Jr. *500 Nations*. New York, NY: Alfred A. Knopf, 1994.

Ketchum, Richard M. *The Winter Soldiers*. New York: Doubleday, 1973.

Langguth, A.J. *Patriots: The Men Who Started the American Revolution*. New York, NY: Simon and Schuster, 1988.

Lancaster, Bruce, Narrative; Ketchum, Richard, M., Editor in Charge. *The American Heritage History of The American Revolution*. New York, NY: American Heritage Publishing Co., Inc., 1958

McCullough, David. *John Adams*. New York, NY: Simon and Schuster, 2001.

Middlekauf, Robert. *The Glorious Cause: The American Revolution, 1763-1789*. New York: Oxford University Press, 1982.

Morrisey, Brendan. *Saratoga 1777: Turning Point of a Revolution*. London, England: Osprey History, 2000.

The New York Public Library *American History Desk Reference*. New York, NY: Macmillan, 1997.

Roberts, J.M. *A History of Europe*. Allen Lane the Penguin Press. New York NY: 1997.

Rodney, Caesar. *Last Will and Testament July 13, 1784*. Kent County Court House. Delaware Public Archives August 17, 1998.

Ryden , George Herbert, (Ed.). *Letters to and from Caesar Rodney, 1756-1784*. Philadelphia, PA: University of Pennsylvania Press, 1933.

Stryker, William S. *The Battles of Trenton and Princeton*. Boston, MA, and New York, NY: Houghton Miflin and Company ; The Riverside Press (Cambridge), 1898

Yoder, Carolyn, P. (Ed.) *George Washington, The Writer*. Honesdale, PA: Boyds Mills Press, 2003

INDEX